PHOTO

PRESIDENT OF THE

THE UNITE

SAVE
AMERICA
PRESIDENT DONALD J. TRUMP
TEXT OHIO TO 88022

SEAL OF THE PRESIDENT OF THE UNITED STATES

TRUMP
TEXT "TRUMP" to 88022
St. Louis, Missouri
MAKE AMERICA GREAT AGAIN!

MAKE AMERICA
MAKE AMERICA

MAKE AMERICA
GREAT AGAIN

MAKE AMERICA
GREAT AGAIN

OF THE PRESIDENT OF THE

Made in the USA
Columbia, SC
24 January 2025

52485126R00024